# BORDER DESIGNS

# BORDER DESIGNS

A TREASURY OF
HUNDREDS OF
DECORATIVE DESIGNS
IN COLOR AND
BLACK AND WHITE

STEPHEN ASTLEY

FIRST PUBLISHED 1990 BY STUDIO EDITIONS LTD.
LONDON, ENGLAND

THIS EDITION PUBLISHED BY PORTLAND HOUSE
DISTRIBUTED BY OUTLET BOOK COMPANY INC.,
A RANDOM HOUSE COMPANY
225 PARK AVENUE SOUTH, NEW YORK, NY 10003

ISBN 0-517-02726-7

EDITED AND DESIGNED BY ANNESS LAW LTD.,
4A THE OLD FORGE,
7A CALEDONIAN ROAD,
LONDON N1

PRINTED AND BOUND IN CZECHOSLOVAKIA

# CONTENTS

———

# INTRODUCTION

'YOU CAN ALWAYS TELL A DESIGNER BY HIS BORDERS'.
*Pattern Design*, Lewis F Day, teacher and author, London, 1903.

THE CATEGORY OF BORDERS is a broad one, and has been interpreted widely for the purpose of this book. This selection includes examples intended for use in many ways, whatever their function when they were originally published. Some were intended for use on paper or in the decoration of rooms, but this in no sense precludes them from being used for almost any application, or acting as an inspiration for designers today.

The use of simple borders to embellish edges is one of the oldest and most common forms of decoration. Border designs can, however, be surprisingly sophisticated, and at this level they are elevated to the status of a minor art form.

Borders often stand alone, defining or delineating a space that is left blank: such borders must contain enough of a pattern to maintain interest and yet not overwhelm the space they enclose. Borders can also be used as a frame around some other feature, defining the space, but not dominating it to the point of diminishing whatever is being framed. It is therefore only in its application that a skilfully chosen border will be seen to its best advantage.

The patterns that make up the borders themselves tend to divide into two categories. Some might be called 'broken' borders, and others 'flowing' borders, although in many cases these are combined. In the first of these, a motif or group of motifs is repeated within the margins of the border, while in the latter a continuous pattern is used. An example of a 'broken' border is the 'golden fishes' border which comes from George and William Audsley's *Polychromatic Decoration as Applied to Buildings in the Medieval Styles*, published in London and Paris in 1882, and Stuttgart in 1883. Variants of what is probably the best known 'flowing' border, the Greek 'fret' have also been taken from the Audsleys' *Polychromatic Decoration* . It is remarkable, however, that neither of these borders presents a particularly satisfactory solution to the most difficult problem of border design, that of turning corners. In all too many cases this is something that can only be accomplished with a notable awkwardness. The abandonment of the repeated pattern and its replacement with an entirely new pattern that turns the corner and acts as a separate feature in itself is one answer.

The vast majority of the illustrations in this book are taken from books published in the nineteenth century. For various reasons, economic, historical and technical, this was the great age of encyclopedias of ornament. These colourful books look as sumptuous as they do because they were produced by a new printing process called lithography. The technique was invented in 1789 by Alois Senefelder (1771–1834) in Munich, and was refined into a full colour process a few years later by Hullmandel in London.

The lithographic printing process depends on the hydrophobic properties of grease: if an image is drawn onto a suitable surface with a greasy crayon and the whole surface is then wetted with water, a greasy printing ink applied later will adhere only to the drawn image. A limestone, found only in the quarries of the Solensfen region of Bavaria, proved to be particularly suitable as a surface from which to print, but sheets of zinc and aluminium were also used, from about 1830 and 1890 respectively, with excellent results. It is not usually possible to judge the material of the printing surface from the printed image although a stone printing surface can sometimes produce slightly richer tones than metal. A different stone had to be used for each colour, but such were the skills of chromolithographers that an image apparently composed of only six colours could have taken up to twenty different stones to produce. The application of each colour is a separate stage in the printing process; all the colours have to be in perfect register i.e. perfectly aligned on the paper, if the image produced is not to be blurred.

The invention in the mid-1850s of photolithography, in which photographic chemical processes were used in the preparation of the printing surface, was a further advance, and really marks the start of modern colour printing. Photolithography was only one of many attempts to introduce photographic techniques into printing. Almost all of them failed to prosper, and some we now know by name only, the actual technique having been lost.

The result of these inventions and their refinements was that colour printing became cheap enough to make a commercial proposition out of producing books with a high number of colour illustrations. Prior to this, prints had to be hand coloured, a slow, labour intensive, and, for publishers printing large quantities of books, very expensive operation.

Books of pattern designs were deemed not merely desirable but necessary as a direct consequence of the industrial revolution. The dramatically increased mechanization of production meant that items that had once been luxury goods and status symbols were now available to a much wider section of society. The newly urbanized and industrialized populations constituted a rapidly growing market for new products. Indeed it was a source of much pride that industrialization had brought the fruits of civilization to a much wider population.

The ornamentation of new products, although often a riot of invention, was frequently undisciplined. Almost any, often little understood, style that could be plundered from the decorative arts of another era was taken and applied indiscriminately. This worried contemporary critics, all the more so because the changes in both production methods and the market had undermined the traditional safeguards of design standards. In a typically British fashion, a committee was established to report on the problem, and in 1836 it produced *The Report of the Select Committee of the House of Commons appointed to enquire into the best means of extending knowledge of the Arts and of the Principles of Design among the people*. The Report, produced after nearly a year's deliberation, highlighted how far British design lagged behind that of continental Europe, especially France, both in execution and education.

This dissatisfaction with the standard of British design led directly to the establishment of a government-funded Normal School of Design, which by 1846 had eleven branch schools, all situated in the main centres of industrial production, such as Hanley, in the middle of the Staffordshire pottery industry. The first head of the school in Hanley was John Charles Robinson (1824–1913), who had studied painting in Paris before being appointed to the school in 1847. Such was Robinson's success that in 1852 he was made Superintendent of the Art Collection at the South Kensington Museum, which was later to become the Victoria and Albert Museum. Robinson made many fine acquisitions for the museum, and wrote prolifically on a wide variety of artistic matters. Many of these publications were aimed specifically at the student of design. In 1853, for example, he published *A Collection of Examples of Coloured Ornament, to serve as first exercises in flat tinting . . . Prepared for the use of Schools in connection with the*

*Department of Science & Art.* This was a compilation of twelve plates, produced by chromolithography, which Robinson had selected from works such as Henry Shaw's *Illuminated Ornaments Selected from Manuscripts of the Middle Ages* (1833), Owen Jones's *Plans, Details and Sections of the Alhambra* (1836–45) and Wilhelm Zahn's *Ornamente aller Klassischen Kunstepochen* (1831–3). It is from Robinson's book that several of the illustrations in the present book have been taken. Several examples have also been selected directly from Zahn's *Ornamente.*

The debate over standards of design encouraged by the government report was brought to a head by the Great Exhibition of 1851. This was intended to better the Paris Exhibition of 1849, and was in almost every way a brilliant success, attracting nearly six million visitors. It also made a profit of £173,896, some of which was later to help with the establishment of the South Kensington Museum. The exhibition was housed in a gigantic elongated greenhouse designed by Joseph Paxton (1801–65), which soon became known as the Crystal Palace. The interior of the building was painted in a series of bright colours to a scheme by Owen Jones (1809–74).

Jones was among the first of a new type of professional designer. He had travelled widely throughout Europe and the Middle East while still in his twenties; his travels bore fruit in, among other publications, *Plans, Details and Sections of the Alhambra*, a highly detailed selection of chromolithographs, printed by Jones himself, and published in 1836–45. He went on to design ceramics and tiles, to advocate the use of cast iron in architecture, and to decorate several houses and churches, often in a style influenced by Moorish art. Throughout his career he produced many books, both by himself and with other authors. After his triumphant colour scheme for the Crystal Palace, he issued *The Grammar of Ornament*, published by Day & Co in 1856. This consisted of one hundred chromolithographed plates concerned with the principles of design, with texts by various collaborators. It soon established itself as a publication of international importance to the design community. International and historical in scope, its quality can be judged from the borders included in this volume taken from Chinese ceramics. Jones went on to demonstrate his versatility as a designer by designing successful wallpapers, textiles, silks, furniture, carpets, interiors both private or domestic and public (including rooms for the South Kensington Museum), silver, metalwork, and even biscuit labels for Huntley & Palmer. Books continued to be an important part of his work, and in 1867 he published *Examples of Chinese Ornament.* It was through books such as these that Jones left us his most important legacy, a wider appreciation of the potential of non-European ornament, and the systematic study of the principles of design.

We have seen how, in almost every way, the Great Exhibition of 1851 was an undoubted public success. However, for many of the organizers, and especially the group of ardent design reformers centred on Henry Cole (1808–82), many of the objects displayed were a source of intense embarrassment. The design of many of the exhibits simply reflected the triumph of ingenuity over everything else, especially style and function: some of them even teetered on the edge of kitsch. For Cole and his circle, these objects typified the extravagant use of ill-understood decoration and ornament that they had been campaigning against.

The design reformers acknowledged few exceptions, to their dismay, but there were occasional redeeming areas. One was a large group of Indian textiles, full of wonderful patterns in brightly coloured dyes, imported from what was then a very distant part of the British Empire. This display helped directly to promote an interest in Indian design, and some £1276 from the Exhibition's profits were spent on acquiring Indian items for display in the South Kensington Museum. These were chosen by a small committee consisting of Sir Henry Cole, Owen Jones (who was to include sections on both Indian and Hindu art in his *Grammar of Ornament*), the design reformer and educationalist Richard Redgrave (1804–88), and the dying architect August Welby Northmore Pugin (1812–52). The committee also spent a large amount of its £5000 budget on Islamic art, largely at Jones's behest.

The Indian display at the Great Exhibition was also notable for being fun to visit: whereas the exhibits of many other countries were for sale at fixed prices, the prices of many Indian goods were negotiable, and haggling for a bargain was not only possible but almost compulsory. This became a fashionable pastime for society ladies. It is also worth noting that, unlike the authorities at the Paris Exhibition, the Organising Committee did not allow price tags to be displayed.

The Exhibition and the subsequent display at the South Kensington Museum, together with the renewed interest in things Indian caused by Queen Victoria being made Empress of India in 1877, had a direct effect on British design, as can be seen in some of the textile designs of William Morris (1834–96). Ironically, the British subjugation of India proved to have unforeseen long-term economic repercussions:

when men such as Provost Orchar of Dundee had saturated the domestic market for textile machinery, they started selling it to India, and enjoyed good short-term profits; ultimately, however, this promoted the eclipse of the British textile industry.

Another chink of light at the Great Exhibition was the Medieval Court. This had been masterminded by the architect and propagandist for the gothic style, AWN Pugin, then only a year from his untimely and tragically early death. This part of the exhibition was recognized as the only one in which English design could be seen to possess real merit. The exhibit received contemporary critical acclaim in both Britain and Europe. It was a public vindication of Pugin's hard-fought battle to change the course of the gothic revival.

Throughout the seventeenth and eighteenth centuries, gothic, where it was chosen, had been a picturesque style with little regard for historical accuracy. Pugin, in a series of brilliant polemical books, set out to change all that. He argued that gothic was the only truly Christian style, and should be exclusively used for this purpose. This argument he supported with others, on economic, structural and practical grounds. Furthermore, gothic represented the correct working relationship between the crafts-man and the designer. For the promoters of the gothic revival it was one of the great tragedies of contemporary life that these two roles had become divorced. Pugin, like William Morris and other subsequent disciples of the Arts and Crafts Movement, shared an admiration for the medieval craft guild system. Another basic influence Pugin brought to the revival was an increasing insistence on the accurate reproduction of historical design and detail.

The number of gothic borders reproduced in this book is a measure of the importance of the gothic revival. Some are quite archeological, others are somewhat more fanciful. All show another quality that enhanced the appeal of gothic in an increasingly industrial society, the exuberant use of colour. This of course could be displayed to maximum advantage in chromolithographic plates. Especially important in this respect are the series of pattern books issued by various members of the Audsley family. Plates taken from their books account for most of the examples of gothic style in this book, and confirms the Audsleys as the major contributors overall to this volume.

George Ashdown Audsley (1838–1925) trained as an architect in his native Scotland before moving to Liverpool in 1856 where he was later joined by his brother William James Audsley (b. 1833), whom he took into partnership. George was an expert on

Japanese art and published several books on various aspects of the subject. In 1878 he and his brother published *Outlines of Ornament in the Leading Styles*, a large manual of flat pattern designs which was republished in London in 1881 and New York in 1882. The brothers then went on to publish *Polychromatic Decoration as Applied to Buildings in the Medieval Styles* (Paris and London 1882, Stuttgart 1883) which concentrated on geometric ornament of the thirteenth century, and featured vigorous plates of the highest quality. While their architectural practice prospered — they even designed a building as far afield as the Layton Art Gallery, Milwaukee, (1888, demolished 1957) — their publishing activities were not always so successful. Their massive project, a *Popular Dictionary of Architecture and Applied Arts* (1878–83), failed after just four volumes. The family returned to publishing with their most elaborate project, *The Practical Decorator and Ornamentist*. This was written by George Audsley with Maurice Ashdown Audsley, presumably his son, and was published in Britain and France in 1892, and in Stuttgart the following year. This was a much expanded version of the earlier *Outlines of Ornament in the Leading Styles*. Much of the formalized and very elaborate, highly coloured ornament in the earlier book must have seemed somewhat out of date, and distinctly unfashionable. For example, gothic had ceased to be a popular style among the younger architects as early as the mid 1870s. The value of the later work was more educational than inspirational, although the authors stressed in their introduction that it was ' . . . a series of designs capable of being executed by the simplest means . . . namely stencilling . . . suitable for the decoration of all ordinary classes of buildings and for the ornamentation of articles of furniture and other objects of utility and beauty.' In 1911, George Audsley moved to New York where with his son, Berthold, he published a series of instructional works on subjects such as stencilling, wood turning and manuscript illumination.

Another major group of borders within the present book is of Arabian derivation. In the nineteenth century, what were then known as the Arab countries — the Middle East and those parts of northern Africa under Islamic influence — became a popular destination for artists and antiquarians. Owen Jones had travelled extensively throughout the Middle East and devoted a section of his *Grammar of Ornament* to Arabian style. In Europe, the style was perceived to have connotations of romantic adventure. It was therefore often thought of as a masculine style and was used in the decoration of rooms considered to be firmly in those parts of a house that women were not likely to visit, such as the smoking room. Good examples are the Arab Room at Cardiff Castle, executed in 1880–81 for the 3rd Marquess of Bute to the designs of William Burges (1827–81), and the almost contemporary Arab Hall, in Leighton House, London. This was designed by George Aitcheson (1825–1910), who, like his client, the painter Alfred, Lord Leighton, and Burges, had travelled in the Middle East.

France's political interests in the Arab world (in 1830 they had successfully invaded and captured Algiers) led to a widespread and popular demand for and appreciation of Arabian art. Two of the most important works published in France on Arabian art are ACTE Prisse d'Avennes' *L'Art Arabe d'après les monuments du Cair depuis le VIIe siècle jusqu'à la fin du XVIIIe* which was published in 1869–77, and Eugene-Victor Collinot and Adalbert de Beaumont's *Recueil de dessins pour l'art et l'industrie*. This was published in 1859, and again, in a much expanded multi-volume format, through the 1880s. It is from this latter printing that many of the plates in this book have been taken. Beaumont was a designer by trade, who with Leon Parville was employed in the pottery founded in 1862 in Boulogne-sur-Seine by Collinot. Beaumont also designed Persian-style pottery for Theodore Deck.

The first group of borders in this book are in the classical styles of ancient Greece and Rome. Since the Renaissance these styles have been employed in all fields of art, architecture and design, but with each period looking at them and interpreting them in a manner peculiar to itself.

In the nineteenth century, Greek art was especially popular and was thought by some critics to be purer than the later Roman styles. It was popular, too, for its associated values: Greece has always been thought of as the cradle of modern civilization, the birthplace of such diverse cultural forces as medicine, mathematics, sculpture and architecture, among many others. Especially important in the last century was the vision of ancient Greece as the foundation of the democratic ideal. It mattered little that the reality of ancient Greece was very far from a democracy in any sense in which the word is used today. Classical architecture soon became established as the style for civic buildings such as town halls, court houses, and those commercial premises seeking a particular image, such as banks. It was for the decoration of the interiors of such buildings that many of the borders illustrated in this book were intended when originally published. They were usually used as borders in tessellated floors, or painted on walls and ceilings with the aid of stencils.

The purpose of this brief introduction is to provide a background to the plates that form the main part of this book, to put into context the main stylistic groupings and to provide some information about the reasons for their production. Where it has been felt appropriate, a few biographical details about the original designers and printers have been included. This book is not a history of ornament, and some important styles and movements have been dealt with only briefly. Most notable among these is the rococo, which features in only two plates. The reason for this is simply the nature of the style; there is very little rococo linear ornament of a type that would sit easily with the rest of the borders in this book.

The assumption common to the authors of the many books from which this one is drawn is that ornament is something that can simply be applied to an otherwise purely functional object; the designer in so doing can transform this object into a work of art. This used to be thought a very nineteenth-century proposition, although there were some notable exceptions. In 1835, the Select Committee looking into ways of extending knowledge of art and design was told by James Nasmyth, engineer and inventor of the steam hammer, of his firm belief in ' . . . the entire reconcilability of elegance of form with bare utility'. At the end of the nineteenth century, this view became the norm with the rise of the functionalist aesthetic. Now as we near the end of the twentieth century there are moves back towards the widespread use of ornamentation, most noticeably at the more playful end of the postmodernist spectrum. It is surely no coincidence that most of the books mentioned in this introduction are now back in print, and finding a new readership looking for decoration, ornament and their sources.

# THE PLATES

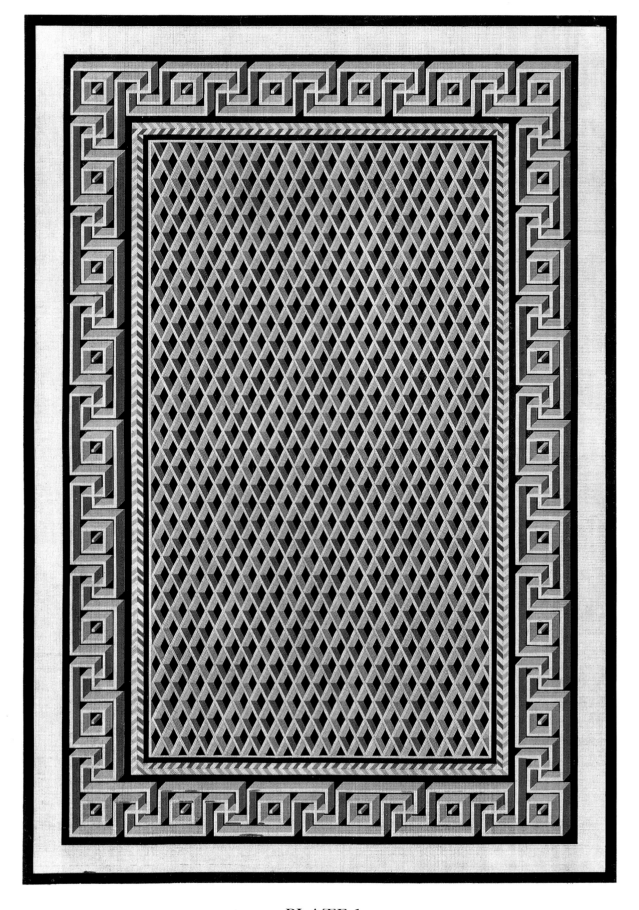

# PLATE 1

JKW ZAHN *DIE SCHÖNSTEN ORNAMENTE UND MERKWÜRDIGSTEN GEMÄLDE AUS POMPEJI* PLATE 2, PAGE 99

This plate by Zahn shows the fruits of his visits to Roman sites in Italy.
This subject is from a brightly coloured pavement.

PLATE 2

GRUNER AND BRAUN *SPECIMENS OF ORNAMENTAL ART* PLATE 27

As described in the original caption, this shows two-fifths of a Roman
tessellated pavement.

PLATE 3

GA AND MA AUDSLEY *THE PRACTICAL DECORATOR AND ORNAMENTIST* PLATE VI

A series of running borders described as being in the Greek style.

## PLATE 4

GA AND MA AUDSLEY *THE PRACTICAL DECORATOR AND ORNAMENTIST* PLATE XIX

A Greco-Roman palmette and anthemion border used for dividing the space in walls and ceilings.

## PLATE 5

GA AND MA AUDSLEY *THE PRACTICAL DECORATOR AND ORNAMENTIST* PLATE LXIII

Examples of solutions to the problem of turning a corner using
simplified forms suitable for stencilled decoration.

PLATE 6

<small>BUSCHER *DIE TONDACHER DER AKROPOLIS* PLATE 1</small>

The volume from which this complex border is taken reflects the
renewed interest in classical archeology that occurred between the two
world wars.

## PLATE 7

GA AND MA AUDSLEY *THE PRACTICAL DECORATOR AND ORNAMENTIST* PLATE V

The flat colours in this volume are simplified and make these borders
eminently suitable for stencilled decoration.

## PLATE 8

GA AND MA AUDSLEY *THE PRACTICAL DECORATOR AND ORNAMENTIST* PLATE VII

These elegant borders use the volute as the basis of their structure and floral forms for decorative interest. The design on the left shows a typical anthemion, this being a highly stylized composition of various flower and leaf shapes.

# PLATE 9

JKW Zahn *Die Schönsten Ornamente* plate II.9

This plate shows borders in a Pompeiian style. Zahn was a keen
archeologist and made several visits to the excavations at Pompeii.

## PLATE 10

JKW ZAHN *DIE SCHÖNSTEN ORNAMENTE* PLATE II.29

Further designs for painted borders in the Pompeiian style.

PLATE 11

GA AND MA AUDSLEY *THE PRACTICAL DECORATOR AND ORNAMENTIST* PLATE XXIII

By the time of the Audsleys' publication, this example of neo-Grecian
style must have seemed rather passé, the fashion for neo-Classical
building having largely passed in Europe.

## PLATE 12

GA AND MA AUDSLEY *THE PRACTICAL DECORATOR AND ORNAMENTIST* PLATE XXV

Another neo-Grecian piece; this was still published despite the Greek
style being thought of as pagan and inappropriate to Britain by Gothic
revivalists, most notably AWN Pugin.

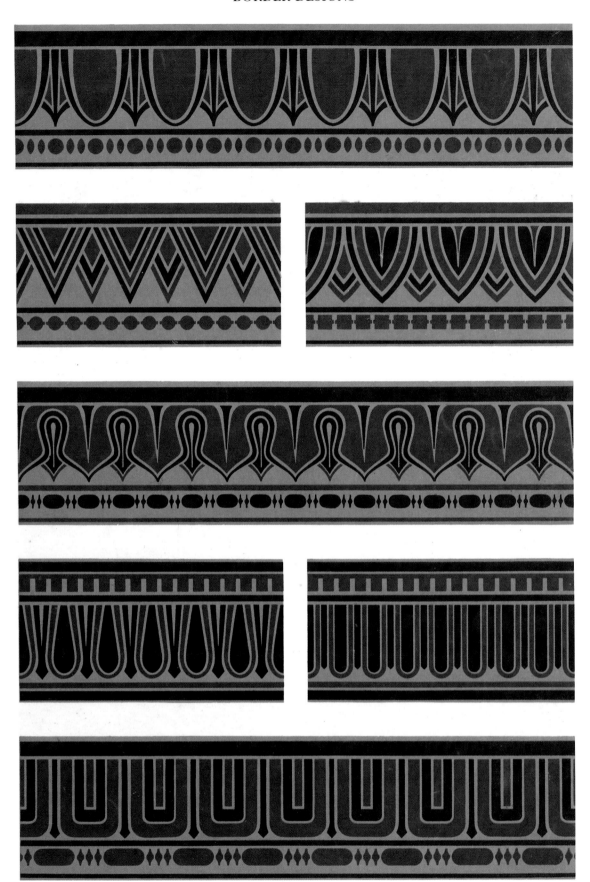

PLATE 13

GA AND MA AUDSLEY *THE PRACTICAL DECORATOR AND ORNAMENTIST* PLATE I

This plate shows the extent to which the Audsleys were prepared to
simplify forms in order to produce bold, graphic patterns.

## PLATE 14

GA AND MA AUDSLEY *THE PRACTICAL DECORATOR AND ORNAMENTIST* PLATE III

A broad working of Greek geometric ornament punctuated by
anthemions in the left-hand border and single motifs in the right-hand
border.

## PLATE 15

JKW ZAHN *DIE SCHÖNSTEN ORNAMENTE* PLATE II.49

New archeological discoveries, such as the House of Castor and Pollux at
Pompeii, sustained the active interest of Victorian designers and artists in
the forms of Classical art and architecture.

# PLATE 16

JKW ZAHN *DIE SCHÖNSTEN ORNAMENTE* PLATE II.75

Three Pompeiian borders from the House of Castor and Pollux, that are
variants of scrollwork, using different colourways and ornamental
features.

## PLATE 17

JKW Zahn *Ornamente aller klassischen Kunstepochen* plate 67

These austerely coloured borders are derived from painted wall
decorations in Pompeii and Herculaneum.

## PLATE 18

JKW ZAHN *ORNAMENTE ALLER KLASSISCHEN KUNSTEPOCHEN* PLATE 21

These borders are taken from tessellated floors in Messina Cathedral.
They were recorded by Wilhelm Zahn on his travels through Italy.

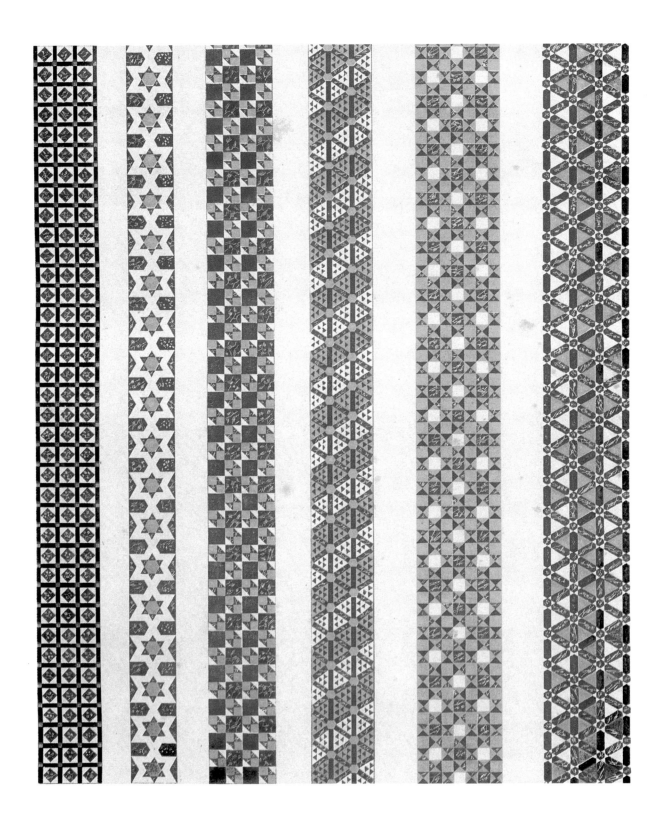

## PLATE 19

### JKW Zahn *Ornamente aller klassischen Kunstepochen* plate 22

Borders taken from tessellated floors in a church in Palermo. These
allover patterns could be used equally well extended over large
rectangular areas.

# PLATE 20

RACINET *Polychromatic Ornament* Middle Ages

These thirty-eight examples are drawn from a variety of illuminated
manuscripts that display features of Greco-Roman, Pompeiian and
Byzantine styles.

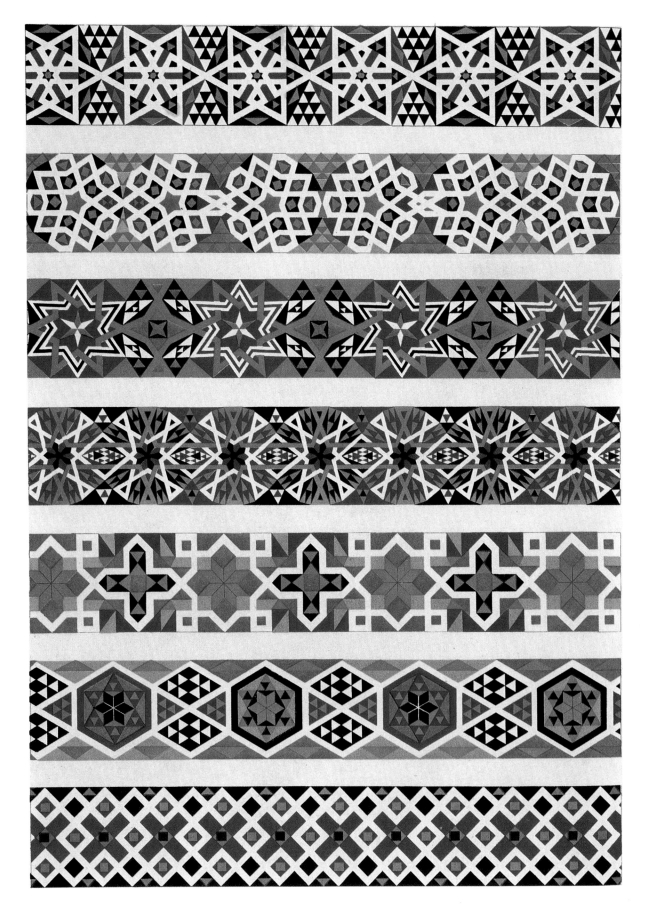

## PLATE 21

JKW Zahn *Ornamente aller klassischen Kunstepochen* plate 98

These elaborate mosaic borders date from a twelfth-century Sicilian church and combine elements of European and Middle Eastern ornament.

## PLATE 22

GA AND MA AUDSLEY *Outlines of Ornament* PLATE CELTIC A

The variety of forms that may be taken by interlaced ornament is clearly demonstrated in this plate.

## PLATE 23

GA AND MA AUDSLEY *OUTLINES OF ORNAMENT* PLATE CELTIC B

This plate shows the highly complex interlacing characteristic of much
Celtic ornament.

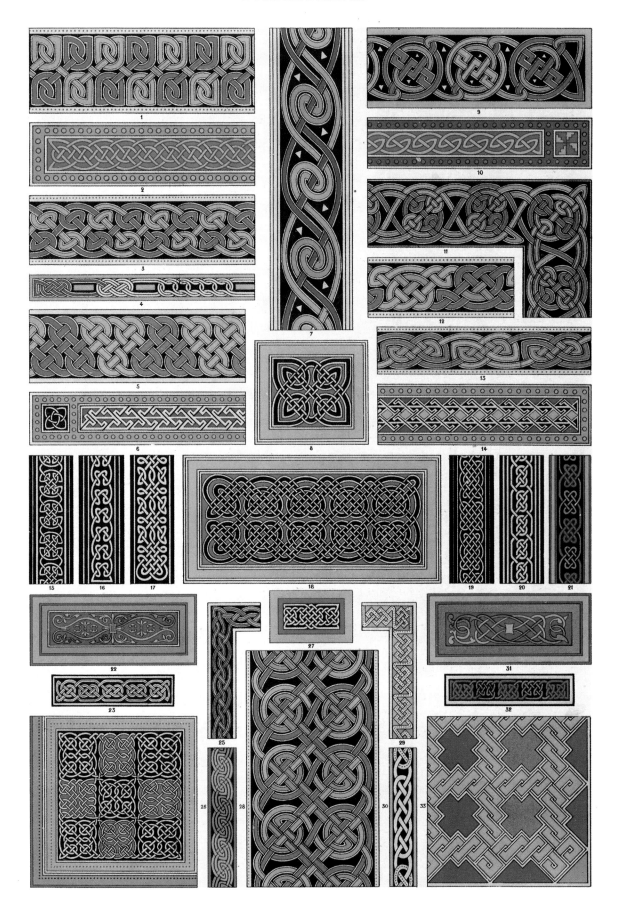

# PLATE 24

*RACINET POLYCHROMATIC DECORATIONS PLATE XXXVIII PAGE 152*

The borders shown here are taken from more than ten different books from six libraries across Europe and include work from the Lindisfarne Gospels.

PLATE 25

BOURGOIN *LES ARTS ARABES* PLATE 65

Jules Bourgoin's book was one of the most lavish published in France depicting Arabian art. This example shows ornament from the ceilings of mosques in Cairo.

## PLATE 26

BOURGOIN *LES ARTS ARABES* PLATE 54

This complex ceiling design is drawn from the El-Moyed Mosque in Egypt.

## PLATE 27

Bourgoin *Les Arts Arabes* plate 68

This plate depicts a brightly coloured ceiling from a school in Cairo.

## PLATE 28

Collinot and de Beaumont *Ornaments de la Perse* plate 23

This design from a Persian manuscript was thought by the authors
especially suitable for application in textile, book and metalwork
decoration.

## PLATE 29

GRUNER AND BRAUN *SPECIMENS OF ORIENTAL ART* PLATE 24

A section of ornamental inlaid woodwork of the fifteenth century from a
church at Verona.

## PLATE 30

*ENCYCLOPEDIE DES ARTS DÉCORATIFS DE L'ORIENT* PLATE 22

Ceramics have always been used in the Middle East as an architectural
material. This plate shows a typical example of highly coloured,
decorative glazed earthenware tiles from a building in Constantinople.

## PLATE 31

*ENCYCLOPEDIE DES ARTS DÉCORATIFS DE L'ORIENT* PLATE 21

This plate depicts another architectural ceramic tile, although the
authors of the *Encyclopedie* suggest that the design could equally be used
on paper. The tile is taken from a building in Cairo.

## PLATE 32

COLLINOT AND DE BEAUMONT *ORNAMENTS DE LA PERSE* PLATE 9

A manuscript page showing a type of stylized floral pattern that became
very influential with nineteenth-century designers such as Owen Jones
and William Morris.

PLATE 33

*Encyclopedie des Arts décoratifs de l'Orient* plate 7

The border of this Persian manuscript resembles the European style of
arabesque in that it displays a dense scrolling foliage.

## PLATE 34

Collinot and de Beaumont *Ornaments de la Perse* plate 35

The border of a carpet given by the Shah of Persia to Louis XIV of France.

# PLATE 35

COLLINOT AND DE BEAUMONT *ORNAMENTS DE LA PERSE* PLATE 50

A detail of the silver repousse work from a door in the college of Shah
Sultan Hussein of Ispahan.

## PLATE 36

COLLINOT AND DE BEAUMONT *ORNAMENTS DE LA PERSE* PLATE 27

A variety of borders from manuscripts: the stylized and highly coloured
flowers are of the type which was to have such a profound influence on
eighteenth-century European textile design.

PLATE 37

GA AND MA AUDSLEY *THE PRACTICAL DECORATOR AND ORNAMENTIST* PLATE II

This lavish design demonstrates the use of gold on dark coloured
backgrounds in the Japanese style.

## PLATE 38

Owen Jones *The Grammar of Ornament* plate LXI

This is the third plate in the section on China in Jones's book. The three borders at the top were taken from painted woodwork; numbers 7, 8 and 11 are derived from textiles, number 16 is from a painting, and the rest are from ceramics.

PLATE 39

<small>OWEN JONES *EXAMPLES OF CHINESE ORNAMENT* PLATE XVI</small>

This plate shows borders from *cloisonné* enamelled vases. The
triangulated structure of these patterns earned the praise of Jones.

# PLATE 40

Owen Jones *Examples of Chinese Ornament* plate XXI

These borders are taken from a variety of blue-and-white ceramics.

## PLATE 41

OWEN JONES *EXAMPLES OF CHINESE ORNAMENT* PLATE LXIV

These borders occur on a number of objects decorated in *cloisonné* enamel. Jones praised the lowest one for the 'way in which the non-descript animals fill up the space in which they float'.

## PLATE 42

OWEN JONES *EXAMPLES OF CHINESE ORNAMENT* PLATE XCVII

Chinoiserie became popular in Europe in the eighteenth century and
Chinese ornament played a major part in the eclectic ferment of
nineteenth-century decoration. Jones had previously criticized Chinese
work but was engrossed by the bright polychromatic ceramics.

PLATE 43

GA AND W AUDSLEY *OUTLINES OF ORNAMENT IN THE LEADING STYLES* MIDDLE AGES [A]

The Audsleys' books were not all highly coloured as can be seen from
these interlaced ornaments, the forms of which date
from the Middle Ages.

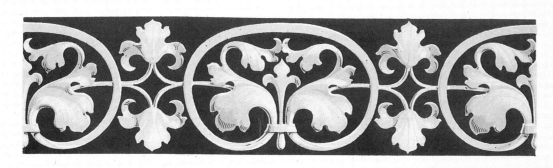

## PLATE 44

GRUNER AND BRAUN *SPECIMENS OF ORNAMENTAL ART* PLATE 45

These foliate borders are taken from the thirteenth-century church of
Sante Andrea at Vercelli.

## PLATE 45

GRUNER AND BRAUN *SPECIMENS OF ORNAMENTAL ART* PLATE 42

This elaborate series of borders was ascribed to Giotto and dates from the
late thirteenth or early fourteenth century.

## PLATE 46

GA AND MA AUDSLEY *THE PRACTICAL DECORATOR AND ORNAMENTIST* PLATE
LXXXII

This type of border with intertwining stylized flowers was a major source
of inspiration for nineteenth-century decorators painting walls and
ceilings.

# PLATE 47

GA AND W AUDSLEY *POLYCHROMATIC DECORATION AS APPLIED TO BUILDINGS IN THE MEDIAEVAL STYLES* PLATE XX

Battlemented crestings for use by decorators as cornices. The lowest two are described as being more French in style.

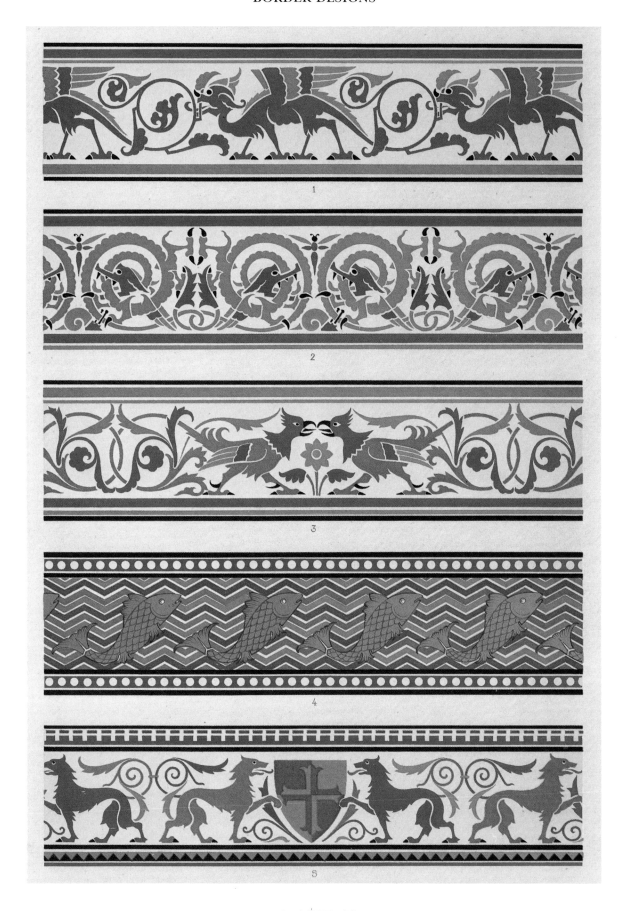

## PLATE 48

GA AND W AUDSLEY *POLYCHROMATIC DECORATION AS APPLIED TO BUILDINGS IN THE MEDIAEVAL STYLES* PLATE XIX

These plates are a good example of figurative motifs being translated into borders. Stylized plant forms are frequently found in borders, but animals are rarer.

PLATE 49

GA AND MA AUDSLEY *THE PRACTICAL DECORATOR AND ORNAMENTIST* PLATE LXXXI

Borders in what the authors describe as 'the conventional floral style'.

## PLATE 50

GA AND MA AUDSLEY *THE PRACTICAL DECORATOR AND ORNAMENTIST* PLATE LXI

These curved bands intended for circular borders use rich colours on
light backgrounds and are described by the Audsleys as being in the 'free
renaissance' style.

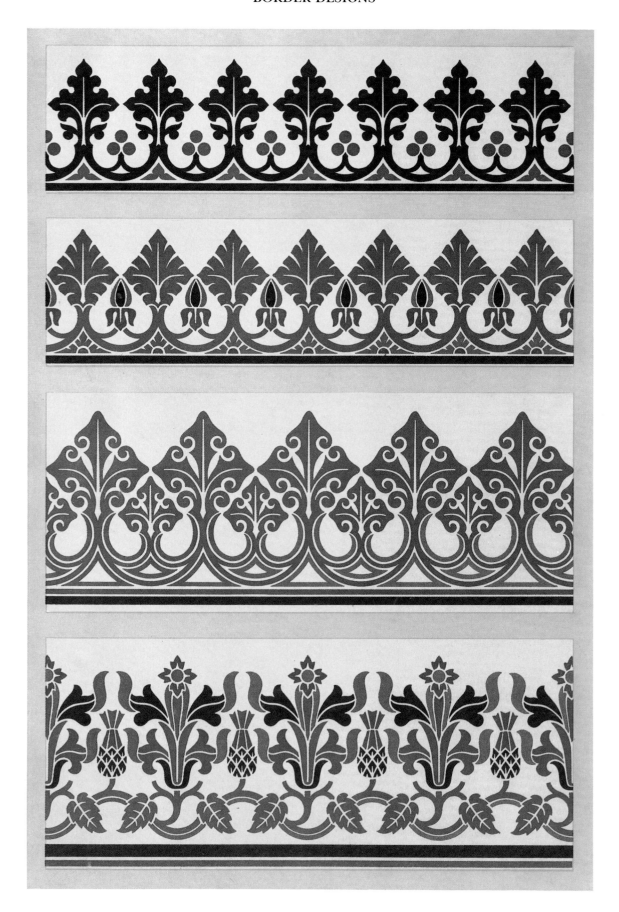

## PLATE 51

GA AND MA AUDSLEY *THE PRACTICAL DECORATOR AND ORNAMENTIST* PLATE LVII

Examples of the crested borders, they are in the late medieval style.

PLATE 52

GA AND MA AUDSLEY *POLYCHROMATIC DECORATION AS APPLIED TO BUILDINGS IN THE MEDIAEVAL STYLES* PLATE XVIII

These are adaptations of thirteenth-century stone carvings in Laon Cathedral. The authors thought that they were therefore suitable for buildings in the Early English and Decorated periods of the Gothic styles.

## PLATE 53

GA AND MA AUDSLEY *POLYCHROMATIC DECORATION AS APPLIED TO BUILDINGS IN THE MEDIAEVAL STYLES* PLATE XV

The Audsleys recommended that these borders be used as bands on shafts or columns. This would be in imitation of the borders at the Sainte Chapelle in Paris.

## PLATE 54

GA AND MA AUDSLEY *THE PRACTICAL DECORATOR AND ORNAMENTIST* PLATE 39

Two running borders suitable for interior decoration, the left-hand using
an ogee form, the right-hand a simple scrolling foliage.

## PLATE 55

H SHAW *ILLUMINATED ORNAMENTS SELECTED FROM MANUSCRIPTS OF THE
MIDDLE AGES*

Henry Shaw (1800–73) was an antiquary, draughtsman and illuminator.
One of his most important books, *Illuminated Ornaments* included many
rare borders and initials.

PLATE 56

H SHAW *ILLUMINATED ORNAMENTS SELECTED FROM MANUSCRIPTS OF THE MIDDLE AGES*

The manuscript from which this is taken is in the British Museum. Shaw published many books on a variety of antiquarian topics, including a further three on manuscript illumination.

 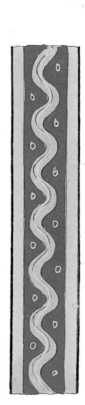 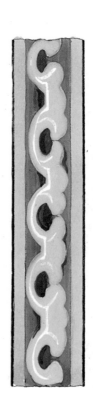 

## PLATE 57

H SHAW *ILLUMINATED ORNAMENTS SELECTED FROM MANUSCRIPTS AND EARLY PRINTED BOOKS* PLATE IV

Borders from illuminations representing a series of subjects from the Old and New Testaments. These are painted in opaque colours in compartments on four large sheets of parchment.

# PLATE 58

H Shaw *Illuminated Ornaments selected from Manuscripts and Early Printed Books* plate X

Sections of borders from a missal showing both interlacing designs and grotesque heads.

## PLATE 59

H SHAW *ILLUMINATED ORNAMENTS SELECTED FROM MANUSCRIPTS AND EARLY PRINTED BOOKS* PLATE XIV

Designs from a fragment of a Harleian manuscript on every other page of which are illuminated borders including highly detailed and brightly coloured naturalistic representations.

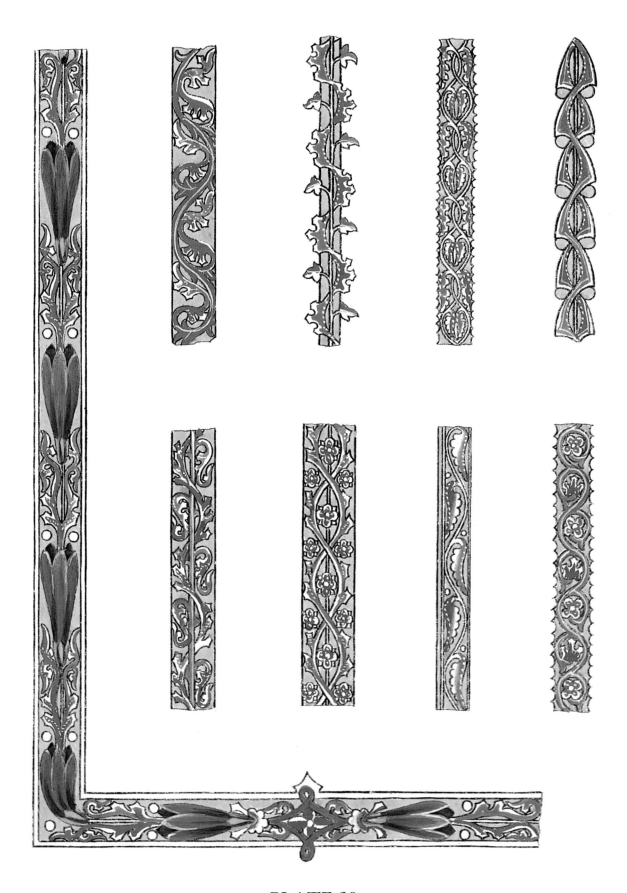

PLATE 60

H SHAW *ILLUMINATED ORNAMENTS SELECTED FROM MANUSCRIPTS AND EARLY PRINTED BOOKS* PLATE XVII

These intricate borders include designs taken from a fifteenth-century French service book and contemporary volume of prayers.

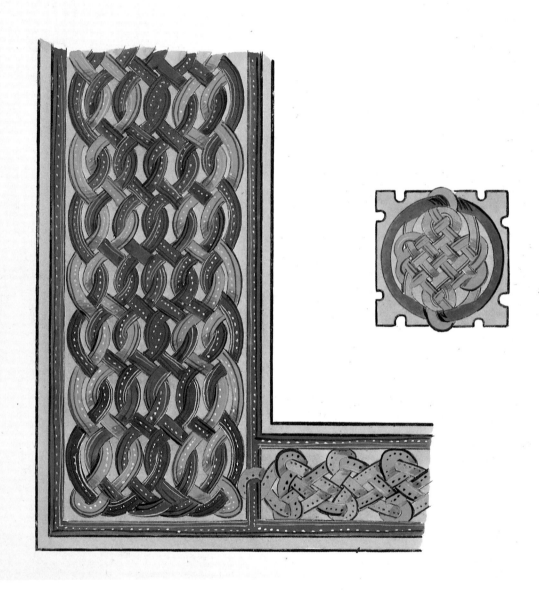

PLATE 61

H SHAW *ILLUMINATED ORNAMENTS SELECTED FROM MANUSCRIPTS AND EARLY PRINTED BOOKS* PLATE XIX

A drawing taken from an early fifteenth-century manuscript in the
Bodleian Library, Oxford showing a loosely drawn northern Italian
interlace and matching initial letter.

## PLATE 62

H SHAW *ILLUMINATED ORNAMENTS SELECTED FROM MANUSCRIPTS AND EARLY PRINTED BOOKS* PLATE XXIV

A rich foliated border from a copy of Christofor Landino's Italian translation of Pliny's *Natural History* printed on vellum at Venice in 1476.

# PLATE 63

H Shaw *Illuminated Ornaments selected from Manuscripts and Early Printed Books* plate XXVI

A design taken from fifteenth-century borders in the manuscript of
Froissart's *Chronicles* in the British Museum. Shaw thought this
unquestionably the finest Froissart manuscript extant.

## PLATE 64

*H Shaw Illuminated Ornaments selected from Manuscripts and Early Printed Books plate XXVIII*

The left-hand example shows the arms of Edward IV within a border of delicate flowers and bold acanthus scrolls, from a manuscript in the Royal Library of the British Museum.

## PLATE 65

H Shaw *Illuminated Ornaments selected from Manuscripts and Early Printed Books* plate XXIX

Sections of borders from the first page of a Harleian manuscript produced in the second half of the fifteenth century and now in the British Museum.

## PLATE 66

H SHAW *ILLUMINATED ORNAMENTS SELECTED FROM MANUSCRIPTS AND EARLY PRINTED BOOKS* PLATE XXXII (A)

Specimens of arabesque borders from fragments of a devotional manuscript executed for Pope Innocent VIII in the mid-fifteenth century. Compare them with details in the next plate.

## PLATE 67

**H Shaw** *Illuminated Ornaments selected from Manuscripts and Early Printed Books* **plate** XXXII (B)

A detail of a fine border of scrolling foliage copied from fragments of a devotional manuscript executed for Pope Innocent VIII.

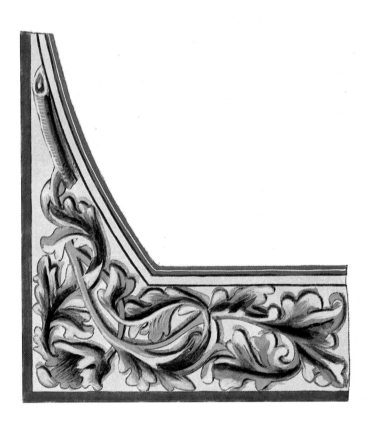

## PLATE 68

H SHAW *ILLUMINATED ORNAMENTS SELECTED FROM MANUSCRIPTS AND EARLY PRINTED BOOKS* PLATE XXXIV (A)

Arched florated borders from a manuscript of French poems in the
Royal Library of the British Museum. Broad scrolled acanthus leaves are
the sole device in this pattern.

# PLATE 69

H Shaw *Illuminated Ornaments selected from Manuscripts and Early Printed Books* plate XXXIV (b)

Examples of borders taken from a manuscript in the Royal Library of the British Museum. Here the forms are 'moulded' by the use of shading.

## PLATE 70

H Shaw *Illuminated Ornaments selected from Manuscripts and Early Printed
Books* plate XXXVIII (a)

A margin taken from *Sforziada* printed in Milan in 1490. The ornamental
features used are characteristic of Renaissance rather than medieval
design, and this is a good example of dependent ornament.

## PLATE 71

H Shaw *Illuminated Ornaments selected from Manuscripts and Early Printed Books* plate XXXVIII (b)

A complete illuminated border from a manuscript page. Scrolling acanthus leaves intertwine with brightly coloured birds and dolphins.

## PLATE 72

H Shaw *Illuminated Ornaments selected from Manuscripts and Early Printed Books* plate XXXIX

Two portions of borders from a devotional book of the sixteenth century showing varied ornamental details; swags and festoons, cartouches, volutes, scrollwork and painted tableau.

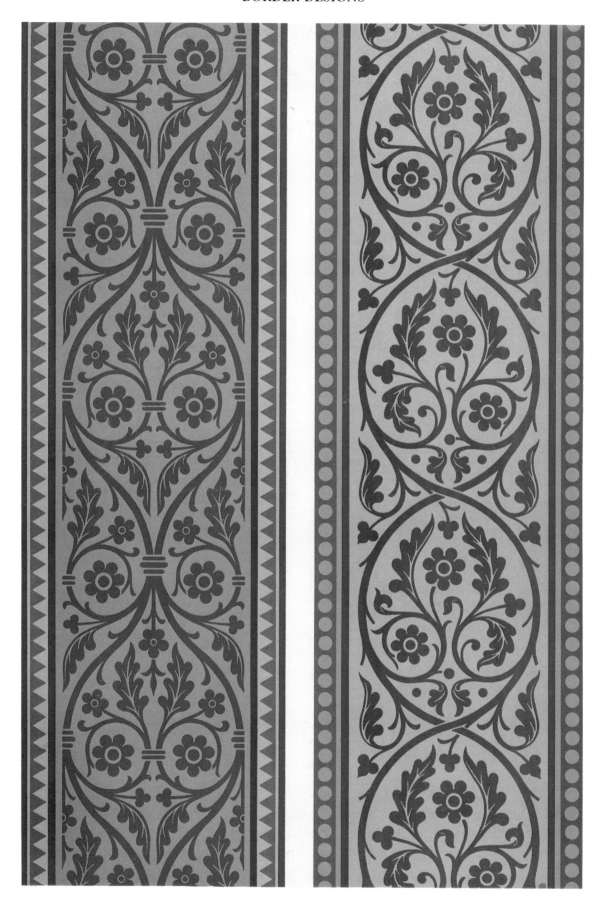

## PLATE 73

GA AND MA AUDSLEY *THE PRACTICAL DECORATOR AND ORNAMENTIST* PLATE XLII

Variants on an ogee structure, the left-hand design being rather more
typical of the two in its use of a meandering rather than overlapping
trellis. These are described by the Audsleys as being suitable for vertical
wallbands or soffit patterns.

## PLATE 74

JKW Zahn *Ornamente aller klassischen Kunstepochen* PLATE 4

The Renaissance arabesque is exemplified in these borders from the
Palazzo Ducale in Mantua.

## PLATE 75

GA AND MA AUDSLEY *THE PRACTICAL DECORATOR AND ORNAMENTIST* PLATE LX

These borders are in the Italian Renaissance style, but would have been
particularly appealing to nineteenth-century decorators as
suitable for dados.

## PLATE 76

BUTSCH *DIE BUCHER-ORNAMENTIK DER RENAISSANCE* PLATE XXXIV

This engraved ornament is typical of the late sixteenth century, in that it
is intended for application in a variety of media, and could be
appropriately incorporated into printed, engraved, carved
or painted borders.

## PLATE 77

BUTSCH *DIE BUCHER-ORNAMENTIK DER RENAISSANCE* PLATE XXVI

The use of wide borders of arabesque work and an illustration, with text below and heading above, is typical of book production during the latter part of the fifteenth century. The style was widely admired and copied by the Private Press movement of the late nineteenth century.

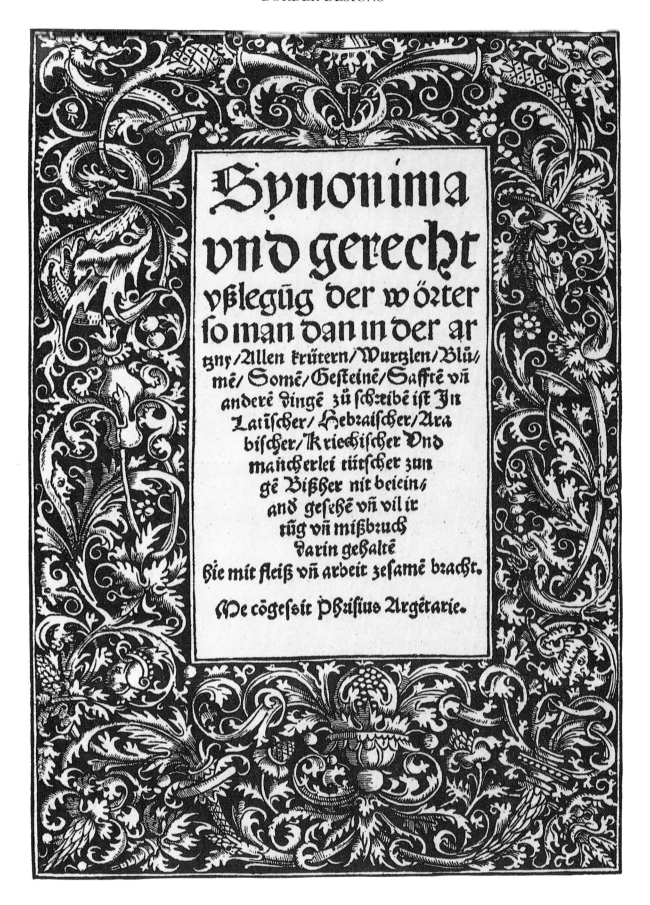

**PLATE 78**

BUTSCH *DIE BUCHER-ORNAMENTIK DER RENAISSANCE* PLATE LXXII

A particularly fine example of arabesque work used in a border.

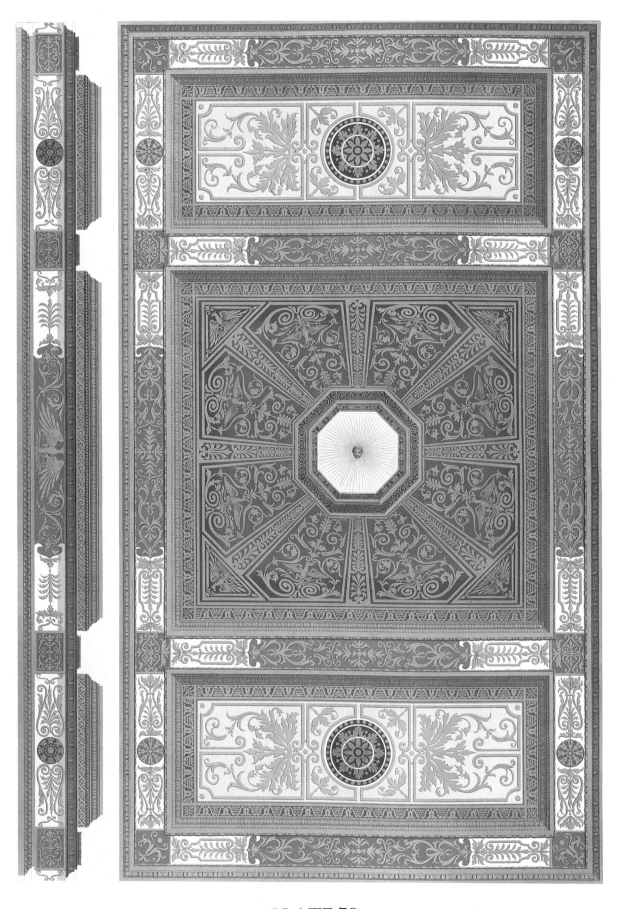

## PLATE 79

GRUNER AND BRAUN *SPECIMENS OF ORNAMENTAL ART* PLATE 70

This plate shows the application of decorative borders in a ceiling of the
sixteenth century. Interpretations of this style were very popular in the
latter part of the nineteenth century when carried out by firms of
decorators such as Craces.

SALVE

# PLATE 80

**REMON *LA DÉCORATION DE STYLE* STYLE RENAISSANCE**

This decoration shows the application of Renaissance forms in a neo-Classical context. Architectural door furniture is rendered unnecessary by this elaborate and elegant borderwork. Two colourways are shown to the left and right of the doorframe.

## PLATE 81

RACINET *POLYCHROMATIC ORNAMENT* PLATE LXX

This illustration shows examples of typical sixteenth-century ornament, including grotesques, strapwork and arabesques. The ornaments in the lower half come from a manuscript executed for Henri II; most of the rest come from works by the Lyons press.

# PLATE 82

RACINET *POLYCHROMATIC ORNAMENT* PLATE LXIX

The borders on this page are examples of strapwork from book bindings
which date from the sixteenth and seventeenth centuries.

PLATE 83

RACINET *POLYCHROMATIC DECORATION* TAPESTRIES

A plate of borders from the Gobelins tapestries that include symbols, grotesques, oriental figures, masks, birds, flowers and a sphinx.

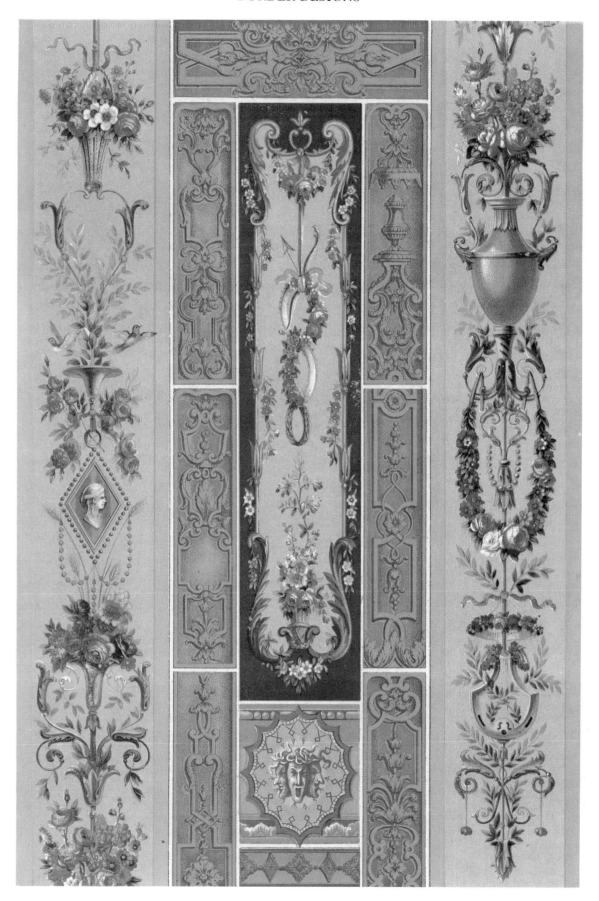

## PLATE 84

RACINET *POLYCHROMATIC DECORATION* TAPESTRIES AND DAMASKEENING

Examples of eighteenth-century ornament including fully modelled
bouquets and strapwork borders.

## PLATE 85

KUMSCH *ORNAMENTE DES XVIII JAHRHUNDERTS* PLATE 16

The taste for chinoiserie became widely fashionable in the 1720s and was
to last throughout the eighteenth century. This example shows two
frames of the type that could be carved and used for ornate mirrors.

## PLATE 86

*KUMSCH ORNAMENTE DES XVIII JAHRHUNDERTS PLATE 12*

This example shows two frames in a conventional rococo style, having
elaborate symbolic programmes; these two examples show trophies of
literature and war respectively.

## PLATE 87

C Dresser *Studies in Design* plate III

Dr Christopher Dresser was a prolific and highly successful designer
throughout the second half of the nineteenth century. He also
experimented with what he described as a new polychromatic design.
This example shows a frieze for the upper part of a wall.

PLATE 88

C DRESSER *Studies in Design* PLATE V

Two borders in Dresser's highly conventionalized 'new style'. He
suggested that the upper one could be run around the architrave of a
door or window, and the lower one used as a dado rail.

## PLATE 89

C DRESSER *STUDIES IN DESIGN* PLATE XIV

Dresser incorporated grotesque animals into many of his designs.
These are derived from medieval ornament, yet Dresser's use of them is
entirely his own.

## PLATE 90

**C DRESSER** *STUDIES IN DESIGN* PLATE LVII

Dresser's experiments led him to adapt existing styles in a quite radical
manner. These two borders are described by him as being in the
gothic style, and he suggested that they be used for friezes in small rooms
or for dado rails.

## PLATE 91

*MAW AND CO CATALOGUE*

Late nineteenth-century fireplace slabs and art tiles, both ornamental
and representational. Picture tiles became extremely popular as advances
in technology allowed them to be printed rather than painted.

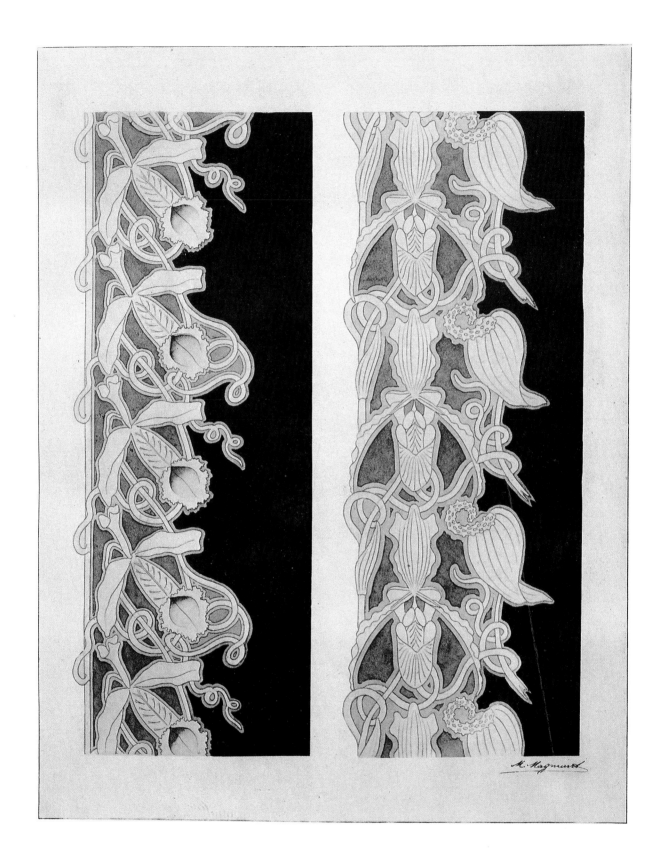

## PLATE 92

Magniant *Fantasies Florales* plate 13

The cursive style of Art Nouveau drew its inspiration from organic
forms. These borders incorporate the plants Loelia tenebrosa and
cypripedium.

# PLATE 93

MAGNIANT *FANTASIES FLORALES* PLATE 8

Various flowers including violets and lilies are developed into linear
repeat designs.

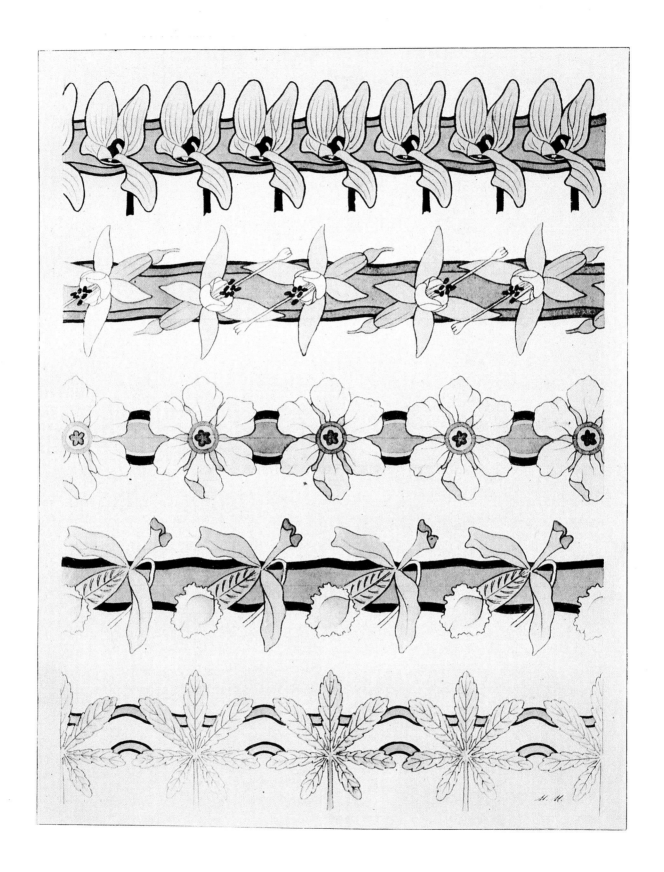

# PLATE 94

MAGNIANT *FANTASIES FLORALES* PLATE 3

Cyclamen, fuchsia and narcissus are among the flowers repeated along
these plain borders. Here the design is dependent simply upon the
reiteration of a single motif.

## PLATE 95

*ALBUM DE LA DÉCORATION* (SERIES 1) PLATE 7

These examples are typical of the process of Art Nouveau pattern
making, in that the observed botanical drawing is then adapted into
abstract pattern.

PLATE 96

*ALBUM DE LA DÉCORATION* (SERIES 3) PLATE 47

In this plate the artist Henri Gillet juxtaposes a variety of insects chosen
for their naturally decorative appearance. The composite nature of the
plate and the more generic patterns anticipate Art Deco publications.

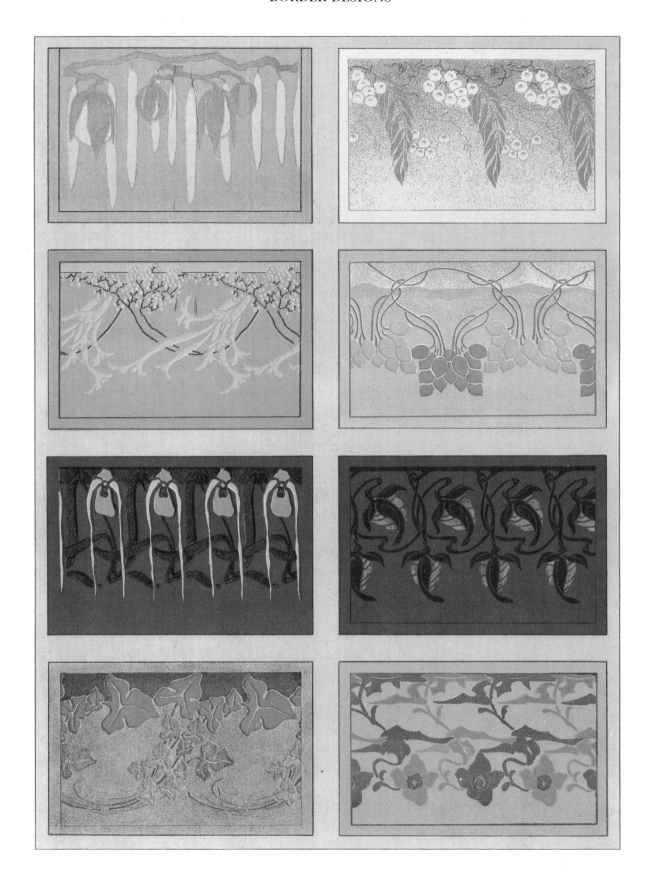

## PLATE 97

*ALBUM DE LA DÉCORATION* (SERIES 3) PLATE 24

Henri Simmen contributed these Art Nouveau borders to this album.
The range of colours and tones on a single page is far wider than in most
Art Nouveau pattern source books.

## PLATE 98

*ALBUM DE LA DÉCORATION* (SERIES 3) PLATE 31

This aquatic border surrounds a quintessentially Art Nouveau water nymph. Picture and border are interdependent, designed as an ornamental tableau by Maurice Duflo.

## PLATE 99

*ALBUM DE LA DÉCORATION* (SERIES 3) PLATE 22

Paul Guignebault designed these Art Nouveau seat covers and borders.

## PLATE 100

Thomas *Formes et Couleurs* plate 6

In the 1920s, textiles and decorative fabrics began to display patterns of
broad dynamic forms in vibrant, saturated colour. These three examples
illustrate well the way in which the Art Deco eye focussed on the angular
rather than the sinuous elements of an organic subject matter.

## PLATE 101

### EA Seguy *Papillons* plate 20

Seguy began his career as a designer of pattern books based on plant
forms in an Art Nouveau style. Gradually he moved towards a more Art
Deco style as can be seen in this example from 1927 which plays very
cleverly on the potential for repeat pattern .

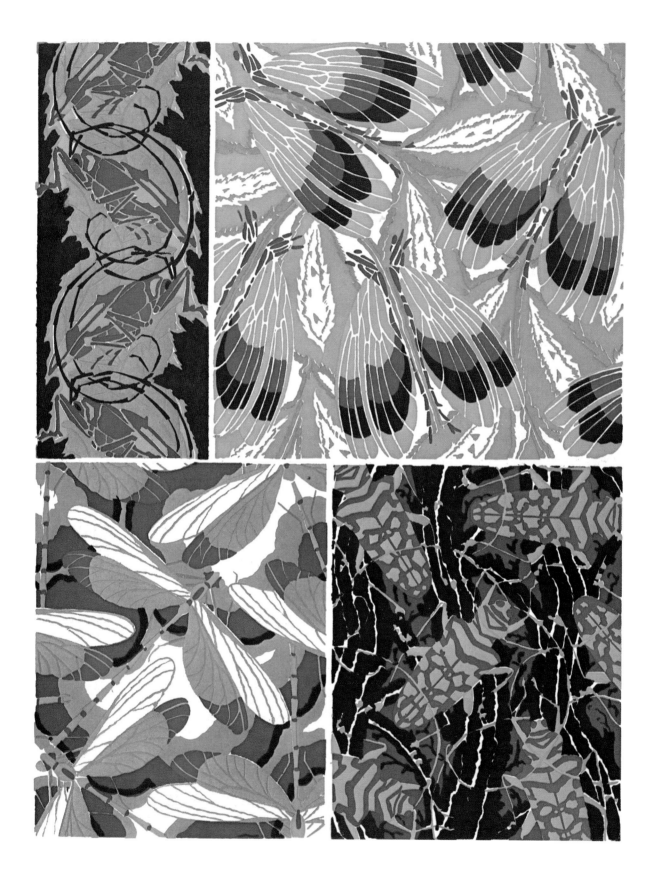

PLATE 102

EA Seguy *Insectes* plate 17

In the top left-hand design based on the forms of locusts, the artist makes
the brittle exoskeleton of the insect the basis for his handling of the
scrolling pattern.

## PLATE 103

**BENEDICTUS** *VARIATIONS* **PLATE** 15

The fact that these borders are repeat designs is carefully masked by the
use of bright, varied colours and dynamic abstract forms.

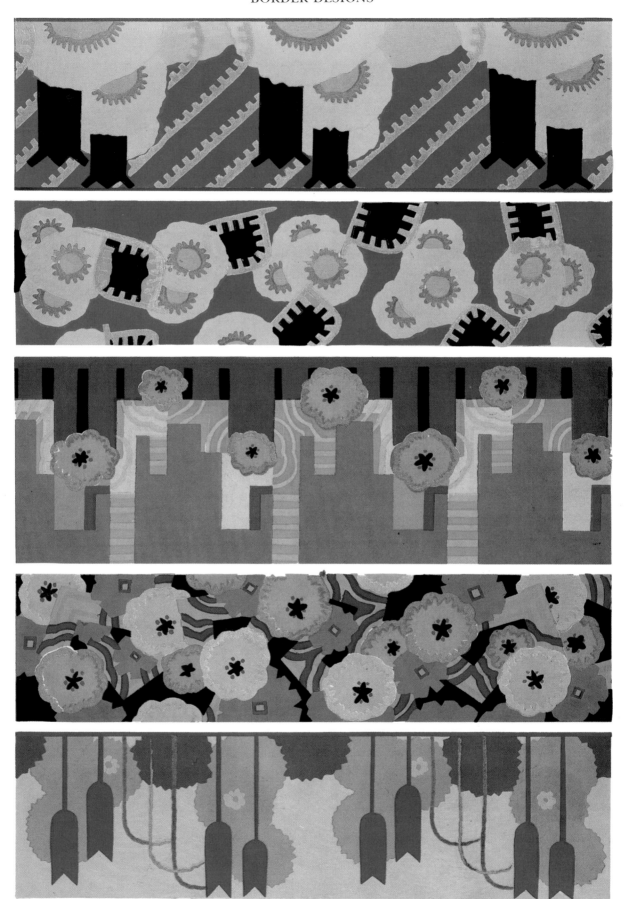

## PLATE 104

*STUDIO D'ARTS DÉCORATIFS* (SERIES 5) PLATE 1

The *Studio d'Arts Décoratifs* was a serial publication aimed at textile
designers and manufacturers. These borders show an
integration of geometric and floral forms peculiar to French printed
patterns of the twenties.

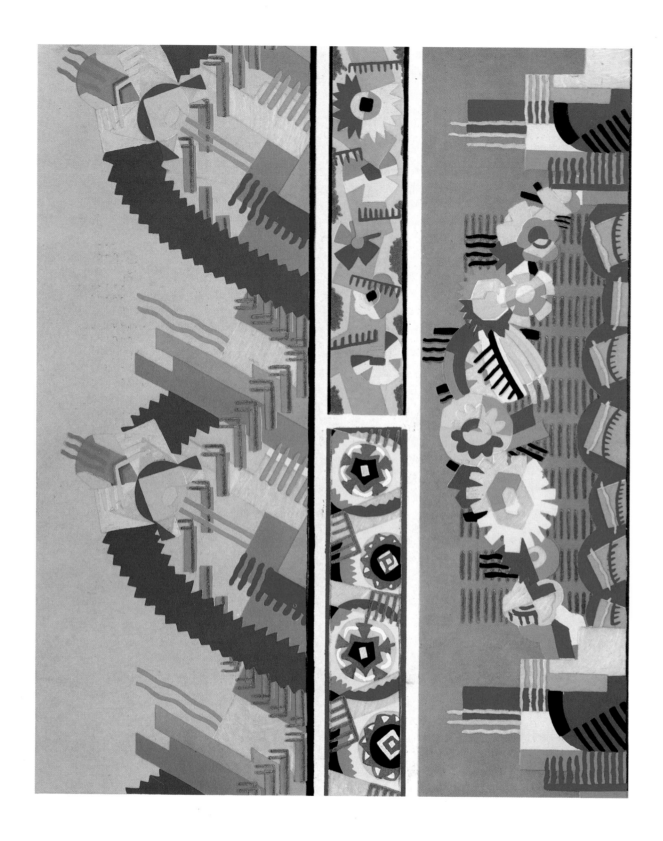

# PLATE 105

*STUDIO D'ARTS DÉCORATIFS* (SERIES 5) PLATE 4

Four abstracted Art Deco patterns. The left-hand panel shows a witty
adaptation of that most classical of ornaments, the festoon. The
treatment of the whole shows a developed response to fine art
movements of the period, most notably Synthetic Cubism.

PLATE 106

*STUDIO D'ARTS DÉCORATIFS* (SERIES 5) PLATE 12

Abstract border designs are here used to frame stylized bouquets. It is
revealing to compare the treatment of this framed subject with others
from the period.

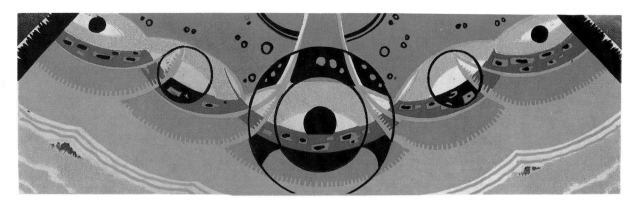

# PLATE 107

*STUDIO D'ARTS DÉCORATIFS* (SERIES 5) PLATE 7

Geometric, almost Futuristic, Art Deco patterns particularly suitable for
printing onto cottons.

## PLATE 108

*STUDIO D'ARTS DÉCORATIFS* (SERIES 5) PLATE 3

An abstract monochrome design influenced by the forms of both analytic
and synthetic cubism. In keeping with the style of the *Studio* publication
this radical Art Deco treatment is punctuated by two floral motifs.

## PLATE 109

*ALBUM DE LA DÉCORATION* PLATE 34

These friezes exploit an equivocation between two-dimensional and
three-dimensional space. Flat forms and broad coloured lines
stress the surface pattern, while the use of overlap and recession creates
an illusion of depth.

# PLATE 110

Bohla *Neue Motive für moderne Flächenverzienung* plates 2, 7, 8, 20

The floral borders are neither wholly Nouveau nor Deco, incorporating
both sinuous line and broad, non-naturalistic areas of bright colour.

# LIST OF PLATES

# BORDER DESIGNS

# BORDER DESIGNS